THE COLD AND THE RUST

THE COLD AND THE RUST

Emily Van Kley

A Karen and Michael Braziller Book
PERSEA BOOKS / NEW YORK

Persea Books, Inc.
277 Broadway
New York, New York 10007

Library of Congress Cataloging-in-Publication Data
Names: Van Kley, Emily, author.
Title: The cold & the rust / Emily Van Kley.
Other titles: Cold and the rust
Description: First edition. | New York : Persea Books, [2018] | "A Karen & Michael Braziller book." | Includes bibliographical references.
Identifiers: LCCN 2017025826 | ISBN 9780892554881 (softcover : acid-free paper)
Classification: LCC PS3622.A5854939 A6 2018 | DDC 811/.6—dc23
LC record available at https://lccn.loc.gov/2017025826

Book design and composition by Rita Lascaro
Typeset in Janson
Manufactured in the United States of America.
Printed on acid-free paper

For Lucia Perillo (1958–2016), whose mind was a marvel

CONTENTS

II.

III.

ACKNOWLEDGMENTS

Many thanks to the following publications in which some of these poems first appeared, occasionally in slightly different forms:

Best New Poets 2013: "Physical Education"
Crab Orchard Review: "Lacustrine"
Essay Daily: "Aurora" (included in "On Distance")
The Florida Review: "Last of the Month," "Vital Signs"
The Iowa Review: "After Winter," "Menstrual," "My Dead Grandfather," "Premises," "You Aren't Sure & I May Not"
Knockout Literary Magazine: "Rules of the Game"
The Mississippi Review: "Not in the Same Way Again"
Nimrod: "Superior," "Until the Heavens Ring," "Varsity Athletics"
Prairie Schooner: "Spitshine"
The Way North: Upper Michigan New Works, Ron Riekki, ed. "Ways to Hunt Deer"

"My Dead Grandfather" was reprinted on *The Far Field.*

"Not in the Same Way Again" was reprinted in *Floating Bridge Review* n. 7, 2014.

"Vital Signs" and "You Aren't Sure & I May Not" were reprinted in *Here: Women Writing on Michigan's Upper Peninsula,* Ron Riekki, ed. (East Lansing: Michigan State UP, 2015).

"Weight Training" was reprinted in *Discoveries: New Writing from the Iowa Review,* Russell Scott Valentino, ed. (Iowa City: Iowa UP: 2012).

I also owe a debt of gratitude to the following, without whom this book may not have come to be:

To G. L. Grey, who understands the order of things.

To Michael Hoeye and Martha Banyas, for residencies at the Far Lookout, where much of this manuscript was (re)written.

To fellow writers and artists who have been generous with time, insight, and commiseration: Poemlookers, my 30/30 cohort, members of Team Awesome, Mykhiel Madrone, and more.

To Brenda Shaughnessy, Claudia Rankine, and the editors of the *Florida Review*, who rocked my raft of self-doubt by choosing some of these poems for distinction—thank you. And wow.

To Gabriel Fried and everyone at Persea Books for their kindness and attention to each detail.

To Greg Spatz and Jonathan Johnson for huge support.

To my family, for believing words are worth it.

To the steadfast and venturesome Allison Eby, for love that helps hold me together.

THE COLD AND THE RUST

I.

VITAL SIGNS

Of many hometowns, this is the bleakest: main street
gap-toothed with abandoned buildings, three restaurants,
two gas stations, hockey rink, bakery, lakeside foodstore
where there may or may not be potatoes

at the end of a dust-scarved shelf. There are those of us
who drink ourselves to death and those who take a lighter hand,
but even teenagers know better

than to believe in immortality. The evidence is everywhere:
field by the church named for Johnny Mazes, whose snow machine
defected in the close woods, whose helmet split

down the middle where there was no seam. Anne Fear,
whose young body pin-balled the cab of a flipped van
and who woke with a cheesecloth memory. Softball
tournament named for the beautiful Ahonen twin

whose twenty-year-old heart fell away in the shower, halved shell
on the shore of an inland sea. For the misanthrope, there are
Superior's silt-blasted wrecks, water so cold even wood won't rot
decently. Flooded mine buildings thrusting their acidy tongues

down and down. Too many deer make for a starving winter,
which means you, clutching your rifle in thin fall snow,
are an instrument of some vital love.

PREMISES

She drove a truck. It wasn't
a question. Her shoulders
were wide the way they had
to be. The ball cap. The smile

like a sturgeon. In the morning,
the white cab with the rummaged
grey grill-work, hubcaps flayed
away on some two-track gaunt
and wily as a lover, ice
on the windshield to say
that nothing we make to see
through stays clear long

or ever. To her, the rifle's
chamber explicable, the gold
thread that pulls a bullet true
amid the red instant of an animal
heart. She bagging Budlight empties
to return for deposit. She back
of the class with Kodiak green

label, refilling her empty Coke
bottle a stickier brown. She Kmart
security in a blue pointed vest, out
in the parking lot brick-walling

the reedy punk with Green
Day's latest slunk in his boxers,
some old grief thing brined
in her chest. The kid's nose
bloodied against packed snow
and ice: accidental. The cold
and the rust smell, the plow-truck

grinding a berm against Old
Highway 2. Oh, she'll haul
him up by the stolen 99-cent
stretch-gloved hand with cut-out
fingers. She'll tighten the backs
of her legs for balance; her boots
with their road salt shorelines

know how to hold. If you must,

remember. But don't go judging
her lovely. Don't go hanging
the winter sun above rows
of bombed-out Chevys, don't
catch her reflection bending
gold in the sliding doors clattery
and fine as a river fit for melting,
behind them everything new.

UNTIL THE HEAVENS RING

I'm a preacher's daughter—
split me open & I'll spill words
dressed up in stoles & black

glasses, clauses fervent
as matchbooks & solemn
as brass-snuffed candles,

each line striving to beat a path
from the made to the maker—
what luck if the difference turns

out to be semantic—oh yes &
the stretched drum of my
heart always trying to lift up

its voice & sing. What I mean
to imply is intellect. Or sex.
But only allegorically.

We are a people who try not
to lead by example. If we
are to arrive at the body

we prefer first to circle back
through a great deal of cloud.
In grade five basement rooms

clamorous with the tooth
clacking of electric typewriters,
it was correct to leave two

spaces after each period.
Now, sentences sit
closer. No need to draw

out the distance between end &
beginning. Only the thumb
still sometimes hovers

over the space bar, wondering
if something more ought
to be done. O the Word

made Flesh! We've had
a lifetime of trouble with both,
already. Fortunately we've learned

to rejoice in our sufferings,
for suffering produces
perseverance, & perseverance

character, & character
a certain feeling in the chest
which might be guilt

& might be gratitude, & which
suggests by its very presence
the possibility of some One

in a position to receive.

LAST OF THE MONTH

On the bus to the Department
of Social and Health Services,
a woman says, Come hell
or high water, I'm making
this appointment. She's not
at her best, exactly,
but she's showing up;
she's showing good faith.
The man behind her, pale
and tortoise-eyed, wrapped
in a pink hand-knit scarf,
says he's proud to hear it.
I still get scared sometimes,
she tells him. He nods.
Understatement
of the century, he says.

Outside the city's muscled
heart recedes from
its concrete extremities.
Parking lots, aluminum siding,
square, floodlit signs. The woman
asks what's his disability.
Schizophren-a, the man says.
Tenderly. Like a nickname.
I put down Stuart Dybek
and see that the bus
is gleaming; no one
dressed in their second skin.

Later, in the waiting room,
a beautiful high femme
sits beside me: trim
slacks, heels that clink
like chain mail when
she crosses linoleum,
bows, eyeliner, not my type
but beautiful all the same.
She's Thai, not Italian,
she tells her cellphone.
Thai, she says. They don't
even sound the same.

The counter parceled
for twelve harried faces.
One calls out Fatima, then founders.
Day in and out this liturgy
of pragmatism. Automated,
narcissistic. If you need
an interpreter, write
your language and dialect
in plain English on the dotted
line. I am easy: paystubbed,
federally acknowledged,
recently laid off, my foreign
grandparents pale as the country
they arrived from. The afternoon
ends with grocery money on a blue
card. And the bus—this time

bright with infants and siblings,
new mothers still holding
their alchemic bellies. Afterschool
traffic. Together we drift home.

YOU AREN'T SURE & I MAY NOT

You aren't sure & I may not
be made of the right kind
of mortar, but how else
to answer the ice
axe of memory, the urge—
part mechanism, part
scarsong—which says return
is instinct & instinct
is absolution & absolution
is all we know of quench.
We go. All praise to
your iron smile & hips
solemn as a staircase,
your anointed fingers,
the complicity of denim
& windows white
with hometown frost.
Praise the place where
I could not have met you.
Praise the tiny city down
twelve miles of ice-rutted
highway, all I knew of
cosmopolitan, its several
thousand inhabitants, stone
courthouse scrimmed
in copper, square-jawed
houses on streets named
Magnetic, everything
built when the mines

seemed eternal &
earth was another word
for *come right in.* Before
the blast that siphoned
an underground river
into the Barnes-Hecker,
filling the throats
of 51, ripping
at the boots of the sole
survivor who terrored up
800 feet of ladder to
the one bright scratch
of sky. Before the new
mines, sliced open like boils,
those too containers for
ache. & when we arrive,
if the people are insular,
if they are hard as the jeweled
snout of a northern pike, if winter
is a shut vault with the lock
cycling & we never
learn to hunt deer or any
more minor creature—
does it mean we wouldn't
flourish? Couldn't we find
a house with cut-glass
windows & let it go to ruin,
tear up the lawn for garden,
watch our collard greens palm

the sun? At night, wouldn't
I close my mouth around
your knuckles, taste broccoli
flowers & the sand which grits
everything, the froze-fish tang
of Superior mawing the harbor
five blocks down? October,
fold us into the creed-cold
winter, snowstorms
like the shed blood of nations.
Spend Sundays in the pews
with the fierce & lowly.
Nights slake & burn.

UPPER PENINSULA

Listen: the place is still there,
you can't imagine how unchanged.

Still, snowmachines gnaw paths
through silvered hardwoods—

one bad slide and a town
swallows its own name.

Beer cans left in the entryway
explode by November.

The dog stands on hind legs, bad hip
buckling, wild for the smell.

At the edge of town, a lake
so big it won't freeze completely

spends winter
pounding itself into sky.

Mine holes like wrenched molars,
packed snow backroads,

iron ore pellets rolling
on the console.

When you lose traction, only a fool
puts faith in the brakes.

Snow is not weather, it's atmosphere:
slushed/dirty

mounded/ pure.
Plowed, it dries hard

like clumped sugar,
covers lust and bad choices,

soaks up food coloring:
green and gold for when the Packers play.

rifle & hooftrack (stretch your eyesight so long it sores, comes
    back recollection. rubbed bark, snapped
    alder. you, again, the purist, allowing only
    what you can carry, knees creaking like old
    trees in the fall-froze woods)

rifle & saltlick (low-tone radio in Kmart plastic shack. fidget.
    piss. check your phone for time & no messages.
    endure grouse out of season; two does at noon.
    when the buck finally comes, stepping light as
    snowfall, hate & love the surge, his trust, your
    need. the noise that breaks the waiting, confuses
    gift with death)

Dodge 4x4 & halfrack (Sunday morning—sober, sorry—
    hammer out dents & replace hood panel
    with grey from the junkyard. soap away
    hide & blood)

RULES OF THE GAME

We were girls. Our practice field patched grass
& sudden stones. Stuffing loosed from cracked vinyl
bases like spores from crushed puff mushrooms.

We ran because feet were one thing to be trusted.
Caught anything that came by air, but mostly
missed grounders that skipped like crazed

rabbits. In the outfield, each head its own
flame of mosquitoes—punishing, Pentecostal,
imparting nothing but proof of where hot blood sang.

After practice, we'd drive to the rock beach
where Black River unraveled into Superior. We'd rubber
our legs into hip-waders, fill chain-link nets with the knife

blades of spring smelt hurtling toward adolescence
among whatever sturgeon the lake yet retained. One of us
was sleeping with our married math teacher. Another in love

with the town's most drunken cop. Still, certain ceremonies
had to be observed. The first smelt of the season we'd grasp
from our nets. Pass a flask of MD 20/20. At the count

of three, bring the creature close. Close our mouths
like river caverns over its face, bite down until tiny bones
snapped & sang. We'd taste the chill & ink-blot

bitterness of what a body aims to keep inside. Keep
closing until teeth meet teeth. Imagine. Turn
our faces from the fire, & spit.

PHYSICAL EDUCATION

The day Coach set up his camera
you were running hurdles

in the upstairs hallway (the track
outside waned to gravel at 50 meters

and could not be trusted to balance
such spindly structures, nor to cleanly

launch a trackshoe's elegant sole).
Coach meant film to expose

firsthand the mistakes he said you
always made: the arm's drift

out of square while erupting
legs and abdomen up from the blocks,

the foot unpointed at lift,
the extra inch of air between plank

and crotch—transgressions
unfelt by the body pouring fast

across linoleum, breathing up
over wood and steel obstacles,

1, 2, 3, ratcheting to a halt
before brick wall at hallway's end.

Strictly speaking, the camera
was a good idea. Except

that you noticed nothing
of stride or armstroke

when Coach fed tape
into player. Instead

the unexpected grace
of your breasts,

lifting and falling
in slow motion, unchained

to the muscle and bone
of the chest toiling behind.

Those insignificant pauses
in the body's line upward, scorned

by boys your age, unable to bolster
the puckered tube top purchased

on sale in anticipation of summer.
Inconsequential, and yet

plain excess to the body's utility,
the face blank as an elbow,

jaw a gear set tight for speed.
Your breasts lashed together

under the sportsbra's softshell,
floating up and settling back

as if gravity were to be
indulged on occasion,

a little pleasure. Speechless
when Coach asked, *What did you see.*

NOT IN THE SAME WAY AGAIN

The motorcycle was his father's,
unused since '76. Its tires were bald;

its fenders flared & brown. I suppose
what I wanted was to be *hers*,

but still it was thrilling to lean in behind
his bare, tapered back, my Kmart

bikini top orange as the vacancy
sign on Tara's Eat-Motel. To be mute,

to be skin, to blaze through the shutter-click
of a Northcountry summer, blacktop

blurring beneath us, pine trees smeared
together like watercolor. His father

had just returned from a decade
wrecked in Florida. They were strangers

but for the motorcycle, which the son
cleaned up, licensed, drove

as if speed were love
& owed him. Five miles

out of town, we'd turn from highway
to grassy-spined two-track,

skid & wobble but never spill,
arrive at the tea-colored river,

the swollen bank where water curled
deep. There, finish undressing,

slide in low, elude horseflies.
For a week in July, the temperature

might reach 90,
& you could need this.

Summer's end I'd leave on scholarship:
return once, twice, & then not

in the same way again. Until then,
the relief of brick-brown water

holding its structure, a million
molecules H_2Oing

between us, microscopic
flora & fauna living their right lives.

APPARITION

The Greek diner where Grandfather
would take us to breakfast: eggs
& spinach, blue salt shakers,
posters of white-rock islands
that scythed laminate seas.

Once, his face was flagrant
as a gapped blouse. He'd lost
a line of teeth, his smile
a poorly kept typewriter
stuck in the keys.

He explained nothing, ordered
only coffee, chewed white
sticks of gum, & stuck them
to his raw vacancies. Half-
tricked, we thought maybe he's

always had a strange bite,
or gnarled it through angry
living, nicotine. To ask,
unpursuant. We stalked
our coffee, feigned ease.

He paid the bill. At times,
the bill was missive, the omelettes
fragmentary. He was in charge
of loving us but since he barely
existed, proved impossible to please.

YOUR GUESS IS AS GOOD AS MINE

Dinner rush over, the dining room empties
of young families, their skis porched at rented
A-frames, of cold-cowed snowmobilers

& a handful of locals in the company of someone
they'd like to impress. You have kept up

with the plates; now rake tips like fallen leaves
into your apron pocket, let the bills bulk
& billow, take up all the space they will lack later

when counted smooth in the driver's seat
of your iced-up Corsica, before you tap the gas

& rock the starter until it catches, stutter
your brakes down the hill home. Conference
sessions upstairs yet to let out, well drinks

& wine spritzers still to be demanded—wrap
yourself in your son's outgrown parka, slip outside

for a cigarette. In the brittle backdoor light
snow drapes from the roof like a dirty washrag.
The busboys cannot be made to shovel so neither

will anyone else, on principle. At the brink
of what you can see, the head chef has set up

sawhorses, a block of ice. Stoned, he drop-
starts a chainsaw, moves the machine
in great arcs, slips & giggles like a teenager.

His polyester pants are stained with short-
rib dinners. He's going for a swan.

The people you serve say you are lucky
to live somewhere so beautiful. That may be.
You haven't seen the places they come from,

unless they're between here & Green Bay.
You imagine postcard-plains & tended rock

gardens, buildings knifed up like broken icicles,
so much height & breadth. Here all but the big lake
is bounded. Jackpines finger even the edges

of your dreams. The chef with whom you mince
words gave your son his thin, mistaken shoulders.

At times it is necessary to approximate distance.
The moon climbs a stand of spruce & foglamps
the snow scar where the resort has been cut

out from forest. The chef's blurred blade,
the ice sloughing & spraying: what to say

of the bird that begins to emerge,
crook-necked, flightless, the pocketknife
the man unfolds to reveal its eyes?

WEIGHT TRAINING

Twenty degrees—a hearse slims
through the blue-dim snow. At the gravesite,
the fourteen year-old waits

to carry his great-grandmother's casket.
He is afraid of his hands slipping
in the cold, afraid the ski gloves

his aunt offers will worsen
his grip. Women are supposed to live
longer, but they do not in his family. Someday

his mother will die and he will have to choose
her casket, his own heart hurtling
toward its final career as a broken stone.

Across the pastured marble,
the hearse treads snow, quieter
than silence. The boy's face is a field

blown clear of its usual exile
and derision. He adjusts the black
wool sweater purchased for the occasion, the tie

in its frowning collar, resists
the urge to pump his knees up and down
for warmth. This year he has grown

three inches, has learned the weight
of a rival team's skinny tackle, of deer carcasses
trussed with webbing, of early morning

grain sacks for the family cow. But these
are the wrong kinds of strength now,
and he knows it. The boy tries

for the mute resolve of rafters. He considers
the structure of his mother's hair holding
steady against winter wind. The hearse stops

and subtracts its engine. He needs
the angle of her face, her jawline,
where sorrow is refracted.

Now? he asks, and pulls on the gloves.

VARSITY ATHLETICS

I'd leave the high school gym,
hips bruised from what Coach

called digging. Too short to play
the front row, I'd watch

the tall girls, how they lined
up like fenceposts

at the net, how they leapt
and hammered the ball

past the other team's faces.
The trick was to hit limp-wristed,

so your hand snapped down.
Like a faggot, Coach would say.

I'd step outside and the cold
would be broken glass.

The streetlights would be ice-
tasseled. My damp hair

would freeze like a wild
chandelier around the winter-dim

lamp of my expression. When a gust
came through, snow would stop

as if flashbulbed, and I would
stop too, my hot muscles

locked, a hitch in the small
weather system of my breath.

The moment would suspend
longer than was strictly

necessary. I'd stay past the point
of thighs gone raw with cold

under sateen track pants,
past snow released to gallop

off in another direction,
past thoughts of my mother's

eight sisters—women enough
to field a high school volleyball team

(too bad they never showed much
interest in athletics), past

the storm canceling specificity,
mounding street signs, parked

cars, liquor bottles
tossed along the sidewalk,

blanketing my little blooming
faggot's heart. Exactly,

not exactly. I'd thank
winter for its status

as neither friend nor foe,
receive the satisfaction

of no answer, only then budge
my ice-block toes—they'd be white

by the time I reached home,
I'd have to rub them back

to usefulness—and start
as if from nowhere, my tracks

behind covered over, senses
scoured in lake-effect wind.

II.

LACUSTRINE

I.
The pain that comes with thaw
metallic, a struck tuning fork

in the blood's lull. Thumbprints
mooned in cold-waxed

skin. Whatever the body
seems to understand,

here it has been shamefully fooled,
having allowed sensation

to seep out unremarked
past two sets of socks,

past the boots' felt linings
& cast rubber soles,

having drawn up the frozen
lake's perilous breath like praise—

while offering no protest,
nothing at all, until in the warm

car, under the hands' earnest
chafings, a blotched pink

returns. Only then, deliverance
all but assured, do the nerves

assemble their factory
of grind & ache.

II.
On the frozen lake, take
your turn with the auger.
Score through the plane
of the caught world to one
still animate below. Fish
are wary. The hours do not

have names. Ice cataracts
each cut place, & nothing
moves until one walleye
flaps up slow & stiff
as barely-worked leather
on a bobbed line.

III.
Lakes freeze but do not die,
like the goldfish one winter

vacation we left & turned
the heat so low the pipes froze,

the tap froze, the aquarium
became a brick of cliffed

& reaching ice. Our pets
terrible sculptures of themselves,

orange scales undimmed,
eyes caught bored-open

in the midst of their daily
ministrations, black suckerfish

printed like apostrophes
to the tank's sides. Furnace

called back to life, we watched
the ice begin to sweat,

watched it feather
back, hang branched &

skeletal in returning water.
We expected the fish

to upend & float
like bath toys, to lump

the slushed surface, instincts
decommissioned, hearts

unspurred. Instead they
unperished. Budged

their gills. Cupped tails
one way & the other

until no worse for wear
they swam up past fern

& Day-Glo arch to kiss the edge
of their universe, credulity

intact, no reason to doubt
the heavens would open

& food begin to fall.

MY DEAD GRANDFATHER

My dead grandfather no longer lives in his apartment,

though his last dishes are clean in the dishwasher,

though his leather gym bag lies unzipped in a grimace

behind the bedroom closet door. My dead grandfather

does not sit at his desk and write checks

to black civic organizations with his pen anchored

in agate. My dead white grandfather, whose skin

will not retain its significance, does not underline

scores at the tops of prisoners' Christian curricula.

He neither shambles across the hall for one ex-wife's pot roast

nor drives ten minutes over state lines to make claims

on morning coffee with his first ex-wife. When I open

the cabinets and every drawer in his apartment,

my dead grandfather does not prevent me from considering

the hand-held vacuum cleaner, the two small wineglasses,

the elegant hammer and book seal with his initials, also mine.

My dead grandfather stays at the church where he is boxed

in a manly crate of brass and satin. I am not afraid,

when we arrive, of his withered mouth sewn straight

over ceramic teeth, of the drill-row forehead unable

to imply a thing from temper to concentration, the hands

improbably folded one over the other, the knuckles

wax-museum pale. I am not afraid of the body

which has been through the busted-brick labor

of dying, not of its shrunkenness, its *itness*, its pall.

And yet a grandfather is a notion that does not ash away

like a last cigarette ground into pavement. My dead

grandfather, laid out in a fine blue suit at the altar

of Lansing First Reformed. Myself a child

who has touched his things.

SUPERIOR

Lamprey ribbons
    sturgeon's steely side,

the eel's nightmare mouth
    circular, bladed, a roulette wheel

of teeth. Its first cut
    sharp & painless, cautious

as a surgeon's. No blood
    wasted. The great fish

hulks on. Its dinosaur
    snout & toothless bite

falsely accused of claiming
    the toes of children

who paddle too far out
    in limb-slowing water,

their lips purpled, the cold
    antiseptic—what doesn't kill you

will make you stronger,
    their parents like to say.

But lamprey knows better:
    that strength may be siphoned.

The great fish pales.
      The lake vasts & voids.

       *   *   *

In November of 1975, my parents
      reached Superior: the Edmund

Fitzgerald newly wrecked
      near the Canadian border,

the wind magnificent,
      waves not yet smoothed

over for the approach of a ballad.
      Their Dodge Dart anchored

to the road by casserole dishes,
      quilted flannel, Jerry Jeff Walker

records, everything worth saving
      from the Sioux Center trailer they abandoned

to ghost its winter plain.
      When you are practiced

at the hollowed-egg art of leaving,
      only the inviolate & disdainful

can make an impression.
        My parents decided to stay.

Already then, lamprey commandeered
        the currents of the St. Lawrence.

Sturgeon's reign was going
        the way of Goliath. Paper &

steel. Ore ships looming
        low as loons, occasionally snapping

their steel bones on the water's
        intemperance. My parents became

as those who lived at water's edge,
        who dressed in sheepskin mittens

& boiled wool mufflers,
        shoveled snow regardless of heart

conditions, & didn't make
        a fuss out of waiting for spring.

STREAK

He hated his clothes:
cottage green cable-knits,
too-short undershirts,

jeans that slacked his thin
frame like stilled sails,
frequently secondhand,

not unlike the spring,
outside sluicing away the fruits
of winter's heavy labor.

You might think he'd shed
them for pure loathing,
but he hated his body

more. Only when swayed
by a certain blend of balefulness
& thrum, only with night

to blot streetside windows
& the woodstove, fire-
hallowed, grumbling

its moral contradictions,
would he pardon his belt
from the hopeless task

of bracing denim to hips
no more than geographical
concepts between rib

and thigh. He'd invert
his sweatshirt so the hood
flung back like something

severed, tug his boxers down
& away. Then the pebbled spine
unharbored. The tensed

buttocks concave as kidneys.
Misplaced modesty of high-top
sneakers to allow the requisite

speed. He'd set his hamstrings
to vibrate, turn the knob,
cricket past the front stoop, & sprint

out of sight: parade of one
I never sidelined, so the rest
is conjecture, the snowdrift

shoulders suddenly streetlit,
the elastic limbs pumping
and fishhook penis jangling in time.

Imagine the heartbreak
dredged up to dermis. Surely
he glowed—some ragged

aura hovering just beyond
his every border. Small-town
Friday night traffic: malt-brined

sons & fathers, fleece-muffled
tourists, each face pearled to the hilt
with his incandescent shame.

SMALL TRAFFIC

I wake in time for the job interview, dress myself carefully
in mud. It's a short walk downtown, past soupy Sylvester Park
where seagulls spar over displaced clamshells,

past shop doors on 5th Avenue piled high with sandbags,
signs turned to closed against yesterday's flood.
State of emergency, the governor calls it, and it's true

matters are no better in our minds
than they are on the freeway, everything awash
in nine feet of water, salmon spawning the on-ramps,

my hair wearing its fake-earnest frown. There's a detour
between Portland and Seattle: 400 miles by way
of Atomic City. On the other side of the table,

four faces want to know how I'd manage difficult
customers. I don't mention the regular I slapped once,
his tomato face and three-cent tip on a cup

of coffee, the day he traced his fingertips
up my forearm, meaning nothing, he said.
Luckily I've grown wiser since then. I've learned

to re-make my body into veined leaves of lettuce.
Dirt or rain: I have my pick of vestments (neither
of which disguise another over-priced white girl trying

to get along). Up the street at the Capitol, hundreds
of Christians are kneeling for unborn babies.
The sewer rat on my way home joins them, his whiskers

penitent as eyelashes, foreleg groping the air for a sign.
This is the morning the flood begins to write
its own ending; even the sky leaves off weeping

as a gesture of goodwill. That job? It's a joke—I'll never
get it. Best to stop near the marina and watch currents
festooned with muddied farm animals whirl out to the Sound.

AFTER WINTER

when we think we have borne
everything, we walk to the park to watch
salmon batter upstream, their lips
spoiling over spiked underbites,
shanks ruby-bright with decay. Better
than any of us they understand
that to compose something beautiful,
you must be very hungry. On one side
of the bridge they teem, waiting without

knowing for the man in the dam-house
to open the gate between the river
and the swollen ovary of the Sound.
The grave-hearted among us drop lines
to water. Dogs strain their leashes,
crazy from the smell of meat turning.
Our lovers take our hands and tell us
they are leaving, their fingers
a hot, brittle shell. Later we lie down
in the park with a bottle of booze
and a bottle of medicine. We are young
and are supposed to feel better.
When a neighbor passes on the path,
black hair skull-tight, round glasses
planetary in stuttered street lamps, we turn
toward water. He sees us or he doesn't.
In the starting rain the silvered street
pebbles away into what came before.

SPITSHINE

I.
Ask about children.
I'll waver. There is the tyranny

of bedtime to consider.
Sloshed milk & split chins.

Plastic tortoise figurines
that bruise the arches. Children

ask for buttered noodles
& cartoon marathons; they want

to be naked all the time.
My grandmother visits, does not

hold with nudity. Believes
one beer puts you on the road

to disaster. For example,
the great aunt who at 50 dyed

her hair black & made her eyes
up until they shone

bright as bowling balls, drank
so much when she played cards

she'd shimmy out of her corset
& flourish it around the table,

with its underarm sweat stains
& whalebone still holding

the swell of her shape.
In the morning, my teenaged

grandmother was the one
to clear cracked beer bottles &

overburdened ashtrays.
To this day, she says

the smell puts her off.

II.
It is a sober winter
with the streets bare in December,

the iced toboggan run that keeps
melting down to fall's anemic bluegrass,

the neighbor kids playing
in ever-browning piles of maple leaves.

Rakish, you walk sideways on the busted-up
sidewalk, like something blown.

When you wear the boiled wool
hat with the flipped brim, I think

about having children. Because, my dear,
you'd make a great grandfather:

your breasts pressed behind
two-toned suitcoats, your love of lawns,

how you know your way around a bottle,
& never need a thing in return.

MENSTRUAL

The pain comes at work while slicing
milky lettuce ends,

their chalk blood
beading. At first not hurt exactly

but a spinal silence over the usual
sloughing and glurping

portent of something mustered.
Nothing you'd

regularly notice, filling
the sink with tepid water

snapping contused romaine leaves
at the stem. Some shift;

the gut glooms
like a distant sound, a dog's howl

shut up in a trailer, an echo
of the organs calling their stockbroker

calibrations across the emulsified
deep. Loosen your belt, breathe the wilt

smell of winter lettuce. Take
again the knife

and move it carefully over vegetables,
crisp and seeping, your movements all

query and creeping, until the first
split-knuckled arrival

which breaks in your center and washes
over every striving thing.

You crouch with a sound outside
of language, you brace against the cooler

door. You, pacing, you, swaying,
you maroon the lettuces—

a coworker gathers you into her car.
The pain comes with its own heartbeat,

hollows the body, makes a vacancy,
leaches blood from the fingers

such that they tingle and fasten
together as claws.

The sleep that comes
after, a fleecing, a web you're caught in;

you could no more wake
than rise from the dead.

WHAT AILS YOU

No surprise that her husband
   was taken, his pearl-button wrists
zip-tied in the usual manner,

face red as an organ not meant
   to be worn outside the skin. For him
the relief of locked doors

and a backseat plasticized to withstand
   the body's brimmings. Silent
pandemonium of lights etching

last-call dark with his glittering lode
   of rage. For Georgine, taller than he is,
her pretty face blunt and forceful

as a hammer (she who broke
   the first bottle against the dazzled
barkeep's counter), nothing

but a shared cab and the homemade
   ceremony her fists make
when a friend suggests

she'd be better off—.
   The cab driver shouting,
the friend's nose yolking

her chin. At Georgine's,
　　the babysitter pockets
two fifties no less accidental

than last week's dollar
　　and change. Children arranged
in their beds like place settings

come soundlessly awake.
　　Georgine smashes the shotglass
because it is too empty. The mirror,

for obvious reasons. The hand-
　　me-down coffee table,
because it always glinted

more beautifully under the athletic
　　blues of her stepmother's wide screen.
Later, flickers to her daughter's

bedroom. Nightstand
　　confessional: a daughter
should learn dreams are only pimped

impossibilities, postscript overtures.
　　The next day overdrawn
with sun, Georgine drives

to Little League practice, watches
   her eldest miss everything,
his eyes shut fist-tight.

III.

FLIGHT PATH

O computerized throwing star,
O white bird claw,
O perforate line across

each pixelate border,
O green wash to signify forest,
O mountains' rumpled beige.

O screen that ticks incremental.
O brash blemish of cities—
Minneapolis, Chicago—Detroit

marked by a red pin stripeless,
unfestive: your only prize.
O icon unblessed, I ride

speckside one row behind
your herringbone wing,
my particulate chair

sailing dot dot dot,
each microscopic
thump failing to upset

my infinitesimal drink.
Soon to land in a city
no more maligned

than any other, unborne
by a cage of ore
extracted from dirt up North,

steel assembled here or
someplace where we demand
the same work be done

for less and faster. Digital
me gliding unaffected
over the Great Lakes'

blue ganglion, neither
coming home nor arriving
from it—no outward

change in the image
when we touch ground.

AURORA

Despite its lack of traffic,
the road required attention:

blacktop gnawed by freeze
& thaw, nonsensical

seams of bedrock, eruptions
of maple root to launch

a station wagon, wreck its rims.
Unwitting deer, their eyes

night-soldered. It was always
dark. We always sped,

so the lights were a problem
when they snaked the sky,

limned the edges of torn-paper
pines, touched themselves

green to violet, sphere
to line. I watched

as if I was leaving.
I was always leaving.

So I swerved, brushed
guardrails, bled my tongue.

Relinquish long enough
& you may no longer

be from anywhere.
Some people like to watch

the dark flare behind
their eyelids. That is one way.

AGAINST CONTENTMENT

Today I hate 5th Avenue, outside
funneling wet & moss-lipped

between ivy-throttled pines.
I hate the grey Toyota that sighs by,

oversleek, its taillights red
& twinned as a spider bite.

The neighbors' robin's egg fence
an insult to behold

as are the twigleg dogs
who shred their vocal cords

after each squirrel that dares
transgress the gravel patch

out front where sidewalk
ought to be. Beyond them

the Methodist church,
detestable, its blonde belfry

& neon cross prodding a sky
grey as a rat's haunch.

Even the windowpane
that snares the whole sad scene

is cracked where the fool
who lived here last

screwed an air conditioner
directly into its vinyl & ignobly

surrounded by scalloped
voile. The walls bedecked

with the glummest black & white
photography imaginable:

knocked-over hydrant, lone
woman clutching knees

to chest on a patchy Western plain.
Misery loves company, thus

the cat's first bird killed
this morning, its elastic just-deadness

confounding the efforts of broom
& dustpan, the scrapyard

its rent underfeathers make
of the mudroom floor. & A___,

regarding the bird's dun ubiquity:
Female starling. Probably just as well.

SARRACENIA, PURPUREA,

We find it tucked between
stunted tamarack & the singular resplendence
   of wild cranberry:
      taproot with radial branching,
         sphagnum backsplash,
bunched anemoneic bouquet.

More than any other plant
   the bog's own creature,
         sarracenia worships water over light,
fattens its leaves, gives them mouths to drink from.
            Late in the season a single pinwheel
     rises above lurked-in
shade, dries to a crackle
   in obsolescent sun.

    Those leaves, their labial openings,
veined red & green like frogskin,
   peach fuzz angled down
to tangle the hair-legs
   of caught insects, coerce them ever lower,

    gastric common room of the inner sanctum
where today two fruit flies float,
     immobile, their body specks

destined for speck-less dissolution
in no way more brutal than our own omnivoric conquests,
yet we observe from a distance,
unclear on the line
that divides the monstrous from the sublime.

BIRCHES
—for A & D VK

Bones in the dark woods.
Lamplight when the moon
rises. You proffer
leaves, *ovate*, nutritious,

to the many-stomached
deer. On the ice-edge
of starvation, moose
peel your paper, gain
what hours they may.

O possessors of *ament,*
catkin, bracht, lovers
of *muskeg, boreal, loess,*
survivors among the *droughty,*
the *wind-thrown* & *scarified,*

you are no stranger to *intimate*
mixtures with long-lasting types
such as white pine
and sugar maple, stark
supermodels of the forest
though you may be.

In your yearbook of shed
pages with their coiled
peach flush, I say I hope
you never succumb
to *skeletonizer,* to *leafminer,*

to lightning strike
or rot. I pitch my tent
among you & begin
to feel other than my

noisesome arrival. Hope
to be judged *susceptible
of a good polish*, if not
possessed of *a graceful air.*

FALL COLOR

This time of year there's no doubt
trees eat light. The forest exalted,

paint spilled to horizons
reluctant to indulge highway,

houses scattered like dropped
birdseed. *Unincorporated.*

Nylund's Pasties. The radio
plays Upper Michigan's favorite

Def Leppard song ever,
while hipster turkeys shuffle

roadside, pink heads slouched
as if headphoned, feathers

tucked back in grey & white
norm core. Later, Polka Don

Sidlowski plays songs
for Polka Ginny, his starlight

& recently lost love. *Moose Xing.*
Hunters welcome. Last winter

the big lake tiled over with ice
that stayed through June—

frozen crags blew out
with the north wind then jostled

back when weather changed.
A public service announcement

about rip currents cannot
address my heart, mollycoddled,

buckshot with longing. How self-
important, the notion

that a place can be left,
a person return.

NOTES

"Until the Heavens Ring" borrows from the hymn Lift Every Voice and Sing, as well as from Romans 5:3-5.

"Small Traffic" references the Great Coastal Gale of 2007.

"Birches" borrows from the Forest Service report *Silvics of North America*, Burns, Russell M. & Honkala, Barbara H., 1990, as well as from the entry "Birch," in The Encyclopaedia Britannica 13th ed., 1926.